# POETRY FROM THE CARDIAC WARD

---

## A COLLECTION OF POEMS WRITTEN DURING AN UNEXPECTED HOSPITAL STAY

### JOHN PURCELL

*For Alice*

*To all who looked after me in the ward and to my family and friends who inspired these poems.*

# CONTENTS

# I

## HOSPITAL

# A BIG BUNCH OF SPARE RIBS

I met a lovely man in the ward

He was in the bed next to me

He used to go out every night

What he did was a mystery

When he came back he was always smiling

His face was oh so happy

Whatever he was up to he was

A very, very happy chappie

I wondered how to ask him

Where he went every night

But I really was afraid to

In case I'd get a fright

But then one night he came in
There was a brown stain on his lip
He knew I saw it so he said to me
Don't worry, it's only a curry chip

Then he turned to tell me
That he orders food every day
And the wife, she brings it in for him
They have a great craic I'd say

So I asked him how he picked them
He said I have just what I please
And he said sure the other night
I had a massive burger with cheese

Then, he said, on Friday
She put on her cooking bibs
And then she arrived into him
With a big bunch of spare ribs

. . .

Then they made a big plan

I'm telling you there's no lies

She arrived in at the weekend

With pizza, garlic bread and fries


To finish off my story

It's best to tell no fibs

Cause if she doesn't bring curry fries

It's a big bunch of spare ribs


Wait the story is not finished

I couldn't end without including this

I turned to him today

And I thought something was amiss


I said, you getting a feed tonight?

He said I'm having a big spread

It's rashers, eggs and sausages

With black pudding in pitta bread


This is the very last verse

I really tell no fibs

If it's not pitta stuffed with lots of food

It's a big bunch of spare ribs

## 2

## THE GALWAY NURSE

I was sitting in the ward the other day

And I was bored out of my skin

The atmosphere was very quiet

When a lovely nurse walked in


She looked so cute and happy

I was trying to catch her eye

But she kept moving round the ward

And she kept on passing me by


She really raised the temperature

She looked just like a pearl

But it all came clear when we realised

That she was a Galway girl

．．．

Her hair was brown

And her eyes near blue

Then I said I'd go to Galway

To walk the Salthill prom with you


When things got quieter

And everything settled down

She walked and stood in front of me

And she gave me a scary frown


I knew right then it wouldn't work

Cause she was so young and free

But still we had some craic there

And sure that's a certainty


Then later on that very day

Sure I really knew my fate

As she said she was going

As she finished work at eight


And she never did come back then

As she went to different places

And I said that I'd chance going

And maybe see her at the Galway races


If we met up there sometime

And her hair was in a curl

Sure there's no other woman that I know

That's like the Galway girl

3

---

## NURSE NURSE NURSE

A man came in the other night

He was in pain of course

Then she came to welcome him

She said, I will be your NURSE

She turned to leave his bedside

To check what was his source

But he just started calling her

Shouting NURSE NURSE NURSE

She said, give me a minute

But he got really worse

All he did was continue

Shouting NURSE NURSE NURSE

Twas funny for a little while
But sure he had no remorse
The only thing that he could do was
Shout NURSE NURSE NURSE

The fun quite quickly disappeared
And now twas like a curse
The only word he seemed to know
Was NURSE NURSE NURSE

But then something came over him
Maybe it was remorse
For he seemed to just stop
Saying NURSE NURSE NURSE

I peeped across to see him
And we were past the worst
Cause he was fast asleep and not
Shouting NURSE NURSE NURSE

·  ·  ·

The moral of the story is

If he comes in again

Don't tell him you're his NURSE

Tell him you are his BIG PAIN!

## 4

## MONITORS

I always thought a monitor
Was a computer screen you see
But I learned a lot about it
When they started monitoring me

I was sent into the hospital
To see what they could find
But what I found out in there
Sure it nearly blew my mind

You see everywhere you go there
And every place you sit
They come around quite often

And on you, a monitor fit


They monitor your heart rate

To make sure that you are sound

And write things for the doctors

To show just what they found


They might send you up to cardiac

To do an echo scan

To check out on the monitor there

That you are spic and span


They also do an ultrasound

To check your tummy out

And also to make sure that

You can drink a pint of stout


But all these monitor scans they do

Will be the best for you

They will show you how to carry on

And live your life so true

. . .

Don't be afraid to go there

As it's only for your good

It will monitor all the answers

To help you live life as you should

# 5

# HOSPITAL MUSICAL CHAIRS

I went down to my doctor

For bloods and an ECG

Then he said I should go to hospital

Just for some certainty

I waited a while in A&E

Waiting to be called in

Then after some quick tests

They decided to keep me in

Off I went to AMC

That's Acute Medical Centre you see

They wheeled me down on a trolley chair

Quite as noisy as could be

When we got down there
There was a fair big crowd
Some were nice and quiet
But lots were very loud

Then my very first move
Was to a better chair
Where they did some tests
And kept me there

Then he moved me to a big soft chair
Over there quite near the stairs
My mind went back to when I was young
And the times we played musical chairs

Early next day I had some tests
An echo, ultrasound and an X-ray too
Trying to find out for sure
What the best thing was to do

. . .

Later they moved me to a bed

More comfort, that's for sure

But I just waited patiently

Waiting for the magic cure


I was also waiting sitting there

Waiting for the doc to come

Hoping he'd have some good news for me

And that he would send me home


But he didn't get the results back

And without that certainty

He couldn't let me home that day

So they sent me up to ward 1 B


Now I'm sitting in another chair

And I am beside another big bed

Waiting for my doc to come by

And send me home instead


The moral of this story

Is watch and mind your health

And always look after your body

And get the chance to spend your wealth

## 6

# DOCTORS & NURSES

Doctors and nurses work real hard

They're here hail, rain or snow

I've seen it really at first hand

As they are always on the go


They never get frustrated

They always have a smile

Always running round the place

With confidence and style


I spend the night surveying

All the good things that they do

I never really realised

They work hard through and through

It really opened up my eyes
I could not praise them enough
So helpful and coherent
But also really tough

They are really nice I like their style
But I hope the time will come
When I am feeling good enough
To make my way back home

But I never will forget my stay
It will always be with me
God bless those docs and nurses
For all eternity

And don't forget the other staff
Also here both night and day
Covering all the angles
To make sure we liked our stay

.   .   .

There's security people out there
Watching every door
They wouldn't let you in there
Unless they were really sure

The cleaners most industrious
By God, they never miss a trick
Cleaning all the doors and floors
And washing down every brick

The porters run all over the place
They bring us there and back
You'd think they were training for the marathon
But sure they also have a great craic

The HCA's are a terrific crew
They are really good at their job
They're so good at helping people
They'd nearly make you sob

So to all these groups of people
We must take off our hat

Cause where would this great hospital be

Without Paul and Liam and Pat

# 7

## A&E

I visited my doctor

In the week gone by

She took my bloods for testing

But said my pressure was a bit high


She asked me to come back again

To do an ECG

When they checked the reading

They said get into A&E


I went back home immediately

And then I told my wife

She said we better do it

As it's just a part of life

. . .

She rang my daughter Elaine

To see if she was free

To take us to Limerick

As quickly as could be


Now we are here in the queue

Just waiting to be seen

It is so slow just waiting here

It really is obscene


But hopefully I will be called

And everything will be fine

We'll go back home immediately

And have a glass of wine


I hope the ending works out well

And we'll soon be on the way

Back home to Shannon

For the ending of the day


Now the moral of the story

Is be as well as you can be

And hope you don't arrive back

In that awful A&E


The story doesn't end there

They're keeping me tonight

Going to do a load of tests

I hope they'll be alright


Then come tomorrow, we will see

Good results and fancy free

Going out the door and heading home

What a happy person I will be

## II

## FAMILY

# 8

## ALICE

I was sitting in the cinema

Back in nineteen seventy

When I got a tap on the shoulder

Saying, would you be able to help me?

Twas the sister of a lad I knew

Asking if I could help her out

Herself and her friend needed to get to Dundrum

And there was no one else about

I had seen the film some months before

So miss the film I would

I told her I'd help to get them there

As quickly as I could

．．．

She brought me back to meet her friend

My god, she was a beauty

I watched her all the journey there

Alice really was a cutie


But then I heard the reason

I really got a big fright

She was looking for her fella

Who did not turn up that night


She didn't have much luck there

She failed to find her man

So I had to take them both back home

I said, I'll date you if I can


We started going out then

Almost 50 years ago

We became quite inseparable

And I really love her so


We'll be married 50 years soon

Since nineteen seventy one

We'll celebrate with our families

All each and every one


Let's all get together then

In October twenty twenty one

We'll have a massive party

Sing and dance the whole night long

# 9

## IRISH TRIPLETS + 1

I met my life long partner

In nineteen seventy

One year later we got wed

And started our family tree


In fairly quick succession

Irish triplets came to us

In 1972, 1973 and 1975

Sure it was a fantastic buzz


Then work got slow and jobs got scarce

And we had to go away

And it put a fairly quick stop

To our antics in the hay

. . .

We went and worked in England

We were there for just 3 years

Then things got good and we moved back home

Without any hurt or fears


Twas happy times, it was so good

We lived our lives as one

I gave my wife a homecoming gift

Our fourth, it was a son


We had a lovely family

We did the best we could

We always tried to do things right

As everyone always should


We had some bad and good times

But we always kept our faith

We never ever really gave up

Even when we left things late


But now they are all grown up

With children of their own

I'm sure the grandchildren will give me

The words for another poem


So good luck to all who read this

Just do the best you can

Look after your family always

Take care of every woman and man

# 10

## MY MOTHER

My mother was a fantastic person

She taught me everything I know

She told me always to behave myself

And never stoop too low


She lost my Dad far too young

She was only forty six

She had to bring us up alone

I'm sure it was hard to fix


She did a very good job

She really did us proud

She rarely really ever complained

At least not out loud

. . .

She really did a great job

All three of us did good

We always were so proud of her

As we really really should


She liked to meet new people

And go to lots of places

Sure every year with Chrissie

They went to the Galway races


For thirty odd years

She helped us to live

She always had good advice

And time of plenty to give


Right up to the very end

She helped us when she could

She always had the answers

As she really always would


She really always was well

Way ahead of her time

I'm sure most people loved her

Twas like lemon and lime


So wherever you are Mam

You'll always be deep

Way down in my heart

Where your memories I'll keep

## 11

---

## MY DAD

I went to bed the other night
And I awoke at 4 o'clock
I was dazed and couldn't believe
I heard the front door knock

I rushed down stairs quickly
To see just who was there
I couldn't believe my eyes
All I could do was stare

It was my Dad who left this life
Almost 60 years ago
I could hardly move
What to say, I did not know

.   .   .

I said to him, will you come in

And we'll have a cup of tea

He nodded and said, I will of course

I wondered how he knew me


He said he was watching from afar

He said sure I did well

My life was full of ups and downs

But I was happy he could tell


We spoke of when we used to play

And when we fished with a friend

He missed those times he sadly said

But sure memories never end


We talked and talked for hours on end

But then twas time to go

I'll call again another time

Oh God, I miss you so


I turned my head and he was gone

The tears filled up my eyes

I was sad to see him go again

But what a great surprise


Suddenly my alarm went

I woke up from my dream

I was full of happiness you see

Like the cat that got the cream

## 12

### 1972

We were living life and having the craic

We always had so much to do

But in April nineteen and seventy two

We found an addition to join our crew


We waited for days

Then she eventually appeared

A little bundle of joy

A new course now to be steered


We weren't ready, of that I'm sure

Doesn't matter what you know

As your whole world is changing

Need help going forward and where to go

My golf took a hiding

But twas well worth the trouble

Having Siobhan in our family

Was like a big happy bubble


We still got to do things

But you had to prepare well

Siobhan was the main person

I'm sure everyone could tell


We got on with our life

Just as well as we could

She always got priority

As every child should


As life progressed on we added to our crew

To arrive where you are going you must

We had four children throughout life

But Siobhan will always be the first

# 13

# DAD: ANNIVERSARY

Anniversaries are things that happen

Just once a year

Memories of more pleasant times

That filled us up with cheer


We have them for our birth day

That's the day we first saw light

Everyone we know was saying

Wasn't that a lovely sight


Anniversaries of when we met

Also when we wed

The day we had our first child

And the amount of noise they made

． ． ．

We remember all our closest friends

Who have left this life for good

All the great times that we had with them

And lots more if only we could


The worst is when we have to go

Our friends all say goodbye

On our anniversary each and every year

They'll meet up and have a good cry


But finally every year from now

We'll remember times gone by

Like birthdays, weddings and other things

That will stay with us til we die

## 14

## MY RAY

Twas on the train home from Thurles

She met a man from Cork

As it turned out to be later

You wouldn't find nicer between here and New York


They glanced and smiled at each other

Not knowing what might be

But then they exchanged phone numbers

And that was the start you see


Things moved on quite quickly

And they met up quite a lot

Sure really looking back now

Eileen was quite besot

. . .

Now we met him up at her house

When we visited one day

And Eileen turned with a big smile

And said this is MY RAY


Now Eileen didn't travel much

She was afraid of planes I'd say

But Ray was into a bit of golf

And went to Spain to play


He asked her to come there with him

And have a lovely stay

And sure he said he'd mind her

And he did, I have to say


When the Irish go to Spain on hols

They sing Ole Ole Ole

But when Eileen finally got there

She sang Oh Ray Oh Ray Oohh Ray


Now they're together for a while

He is really nice I'd say

But all Eileen keeps on saying

This is the love of my life MY RAY


So when the summer comes again

And the farmers cut the hay

You'll hear Eileen in the background

Singing Ooh Ray Ooh Ray MY RAY

# 15

## PAT'S ROCK

My brother in law rang me the other day

He was feeling kind of small

He was out in the back garden

Trying to build a wall

Things were going quite smoothly

And he didn't have a moan

Then suddenly in his path

Stood a fairly big stone

He surveyed it from every angle

He needed to take stock

Cause he found it wasn't a big stone

Twas a bigger nasty rock

He tried every trick known to him

He even got a sledge

But no matter what he did

He couldn't get the edge

Then he got a brainstorm

I need to get a Kango

But he might as well have been

In with Bernie doing the tango

But then the Kango jumped a bit

And Pat sure got a knock

And no matter what he tried to do

He couldn't break the rock

He got a few days rest then

And became a fresher man

Then he got his thought's together

To work out a proper plan

.   .   .

But all things have good endings

When your mind you do unblock

So he found out all the answers

And demolished PAT'S ROCK

## 16

# MY LOVELY BROWN EYES

We were visiting a house

One night the other week

And discussing how Covid

Made everyone quite meek

We were hoping that the vaccine

Would be ready soon

And save us all together

From utter doom and gloom

Then someone said

If the worst came around

Would you be cremated

Or put in the ground

. . .

I said sure when I am gone

Don't think it would bother me

Sure whatever was decided

Would be fine you see


The talk went on

And a big debate

If the worst did happen

Would you donate


I looked at them

And I said with a smile

Sure mine are crocked

By a big long mile


I said to Claire

And what would you do

Would you donate

To a worthy crew


She said I would

Much to my surprise

But I wouldn't donate

My lovely brown eyes


Then I stared at her eyes

And sure I could see

If mine were like hers

I'd keep them for all eternity

# 17

# FANTASTIC FOOD

## AKA CLAIRE'S STUFFING

Food's been around for ages

We've been eating it all our life

But sometimes when you've had some

It can fill your head with strife

Recipes are so wonderful

Ingredients set to mix

But doing it in the right sequence

Can help the food to fix

If you miss out something

From the recipe you've been told

The taste can alter quite a bit

And it might turn out so cold


Like the recipe we got lately

It's known as Claire's Stuffing

If you don't follow the instructions

It really taste's like nothing


Matthieu had some the other day

His eyes lit up with joy

When he tasted Claire's Stuffing

Twas like he got a toy


A few weeks later he had more

But it didn't taste the same

Nana had left something out

And the taste it was quite lame


He didn't eat the stuffing

As he knew it wasn't right

He left it sitting on his plate

Right there in everyone's sight

.   .   .

The next day he came to eat

He asked if it was Claire's Stuffing

Nana said it was and gave him some

Oh lovely it's like a breadcrumb muffin

## 18

# GONE BUT NOT FORGOTTEN

The worst in all this life

Is to lose a family friend

But always please remember

This doesn't mean the end


If someone you know is taken away

To some unknown part

Just embroider their name

Deep down in your heart


True friends in life

Are hard to find

So when you make some

You should really mind

.   .   .

If someone close

Gets called away

Don't forget to always

Sit and pray


When you're down and out

And filled with fear

Don't forget to talk

To the ones that are not here


All good friends in life

Whether here or away

Will always listen

To what you have to say


They'll help you recover

And get you back your esteem

They'll always be there

To help fulfil your dream


When someone is taken

Don't grieve for too long

Remembering the good times

Will help bring you along


Always ask them to help you

To achieve just what you need

They will always support you

I tell you take heed


Keep their names embroidered

Deep down in your heart

They'll give you all the help you need

When you are trying to restart

# III

## SPORT

# 19

# A RECORD 63

I woke up on Sat morning

God I might be late

I was playing the July tankard

Teeing of at quarter to eight


I was feeling quite elated

After Wednesday's winning go

I played some super golf

Even got two Eagles in a row


But I was soon deflated

I couldn't sink a putt

Only four pars in the first four holes

I was feeling a bit low but

．　．　．

On the fifth I was frustrated

It was hit my drive or bust

It could have gone just anywhere

But it nearly made the green just

I chipped the ball into the hole

An Eagle now that's the craic

I was now two under par for five

And really back on track.

The 6th par five was on in two

My Eagle putt in the hole

What a brilliant turn around

I felt I was now on pole

The par five 8th was easy

I reached it again in two

The ball was inches from the hole

Sure I nearly had a two

Two Birdies followed in succession

As I Birdied 9 and 10

Life was really brilliant

And I was playing great again


Two Bogeys knocked me back a bit

I missed two short putts for pars

If I wasn't very careful

My round could end with scars


I steadied up my game again

Three Birdies in the last five

It added up to sixty three

Sure twas great to be alive


A course record was my final score

By a massive country mile

Sure it was like all my birthdays together

All I could do was smile

# 20

# THE 10 MONTHS, 3 DAYS, 6 MINUTE MATCH

I've been a sportsman all my life

But I never thought I'd see

Something that happened recently

Will surely go down in history


Twas in September 2019

The game was in full flow

It was a top of the table clash

And it was tough as you'd expect though


It was near the end of normal time

When the player he got a knock

There was just two mins plus injury time

When the ref shouted, stop the clock

.   .   .

What happened then was unusual

His team went to the dressing room

While our team moved around the field

To try and keep themselves warm


The ref suggested finish the match

Move to the second pitch and play

But they wouldn't leave him on his own

Cause the ambulance was on the way


The game was then abandoned

Sure what would the outcome be

We were leading two to one

Surely our victory


But time goes on and Covid came

And a solution was not found

They put it on the long finger

To see what would come around


Now here we are 10 months later

It's like a magic mystery

What's happening this Saturday

Will go down in history


The game will be restated

Six minutes to be played

The outcome of the league this year

Will depend on the result displayed


But the most amazing aspect

Of the decision taken here

Is a game that took so long to finish

Ten months three days, that's clear


Will any event take longer

In this or any other game

It's amazing it could happen

I can't see the reason it really is a shame


The player went to hospital

He was home again same day

His injury was a small one

And he was quite okay

So that's the story I have

I wonder will we ever see

A game that will last longer

Throughout all of history

# IV

---

# LIVELY LINE

# 21

# SAINT JOSEPH

## AKA WASH YOUR HANDS, AKA THE LIVELY LINE

There is a man I listen to

Each day on the radio

It's a pleasure to just hear him

Sure his name it is Joe


Joe Duffy's show is Liveline

He's on each day from two to three

Just listening to the stories

Fills my head with agony


His show is different every day

With stories to beat the band

He cares for all his listeners

Saying stay safe and wash your hands

. . .

Some stories are so sad

They would make some hard men cry

Some people have had so much grief

It's hard for them to try


But Joe keeps it on going

Trying to solve their plight

Getting others to join in

And help them with their fight


Joe doesn't seem to worry

If the problem's big or small

He takes on all the wrong doings

And tries to help them all


He is surely due for something

Maybe a Sainthood too

Because he helps so many

He deserves it through and through


If you listen to Joe each day

On the Lively Line he says

You might be able to help some

Sort out their problem days


If you've had the pleasure

To hear him say, wash your hands

You'll be part of all the people

Throughout these Irish lands


Come on join and help the plan

Let's keep him on the go

Let's get behind this honourable man

And give him his title Saint Joe

# 22

## MOTHER AND BABY HOMES

The past few weeks I tell you

I've listened in despair

To the stories being broadcast

On RTÉ radio with some care


In disbelief I listened

To one story then the next

I couldn't quite control myself

And I was really getting vexed


Then on came a lady called Cathy

And her son called Damian John

And her story was quite horrible

Don't know how she carried on

. . .

She was a lovely person

Who was told a lot of lies

And the way she told her story

Brought big tears to my eyes


Lots of people were the cause

Of the rules that were put in play

But they were very different

To what should have been I pray


The priests and the nuns

And the politicians too

Were the cause of the problems

I do believe that's true


Before it is too late to do

The proper things I dare

Someone should stand up own up

And at least show that they care


It won't fix all the problems

Created down the years

But it might help some recover

After crying all those tears


But listen it's never too late

To try and fix the wrong

It could help many people

Get their lives on song

# 23

# THE TENERIFE SCAM

## AKA PULL THE TRUTH

Covid is hurting everyone

In one way or another

Filling our heads with bad thoughts

Sure why should we all bother


People bend and change the rules

To do what they want to do

They couldn't give a care at all

What happens to me or you


Foreign holidays are banned sure

To try and contain the virus

But some people just ignore the law

And don't really care about us

. . .

The latest con is to book a place
In a Tenerife dental clinic
Just board the flight and go there
But it's really for a big picnic

People book a dental spot
To supposedly get teeth checked
But sure they never turned up
As around Tenerife they trekked

It's not fair on other people
Who try to obey the rules
We end up being treated
Like a big big bunch of fools

But thank God something happened
And the Gardaí were in mind
Just get these people coming home
Make sure that they are fined

It is not fair or healthy

It just shouldn't be allowed

It's so wrong what they're doing

What a horrible crowd


So please just stop them going

And risking all our hale

Just get them on the way out

And throw them back in jail

# 24

# THE TERRIBLE TWO
## AKA BONNY CLARK & CLYDE FLYNN

These terrible two people

Came to light the other day

Of how they did some awful deeds

On the homeless they did prey


They were removed as solicitors

Then they conceived a horrible plan

They would create false identities

Of women and of man


They preyed upon the homeless

They needed identity kits

They offered one hundred euros

For PPS numbers and other bits

. . .

Then they created false identities

With the papers that they got

Went into banks and Credit Unions

And borrowed quite a lot


They made a few payments

To fool the staff inside

But after a few months passed

Gone and took them for a ride


Most of them didn't understand

The plan that was going on

They didn't realise the theft

And they just let them carry on


One guy in the Bank of Ireland

Saw that some things were the same

On different loan applications

Even under a different name


Only for he saw the paperwork

And then discovered the plot

They would have taken everything

And cleared the bloody lot


He got four years will be out in two

She got two will be out before

Three hundred grand still missing

Will keep them going forever more

# 25

# LIFE LOANS AND FAIR DEALS

I listened to Joe Duffy

Just again last week

The stories that I heard

Made me really feel quite meek


People spoke about life loans

And the trouble that they did

Sure the terms of the agreement

Were really very well hid


The terms were fifteen years

With compound interest and all

Sure most of the people didn't know

They were heading for a fall

.   .   .

If you realised and then wanted

To fully clear off the loan

The fifteen years full interest

Would really cause you to moan


Some people were shattered

And more people really thought

That they were a mighty burden

And some relief they sought


But who let this scenario happen

It just doesn't make any sense

When all the bank just wanted to do

Was take all your hard earned pence


After fifteen long hard years

Sure more than half of your house is gone

And sure in another ten years

It would be really fully done


Then on top of this life loan

Some other people did say

Sure just look at the other deal

To cover your health care stay


In some Fair Deal homes its true

The costs are oh so high

If you stay for a few years

Your house value is gone totally dry


So life loans should be altered

Called lifeless loans instead

As it really is so horrible

What happens to your homestead


And Fair Deals should be renamed

Called fairytale deals I think

As your property would just disappear

And leave your family to sink

V

ELVIS PRESLEY

# 26

# THE GREATEST SINGER EVER
## AKA ELVIS PRESLEY

Elvis said that going through life

You'll come across all kinds

But be careful if you meet up

With those with Suspicious Minds


Elvis was a great great man

Who always had a care

And if you were feeling lonely

He'd sing Let Me Be Your Teddy Bear


If you were unlucky and

You found yourself in lock

He'd quickly be in touch to sing

Come on and do the Jailhouse Rock

. . .

If you were feeling down and out

And feeling very blue

He'd get in touch and then he'd sing

I Can't Help Falling in Love With You


If trouble followed you around

And you weren't being too clever

Elvis would get in touch to sing

Come on It's Now or Never


When you're in a lot of bother

And your mind is in full flight

Elvis would be in touch to say

Hi, Are You Lonesome Tonight


When your life is in some turmoil

And you've been on a big bender

He'd be the first to call to say

Come on and Love Me Tender


You meet all kinds of people

But you would be lucky to find

One who would call you every day

To say you are Always On My Mind


When you are getting ready to go out

And you're finding it hard to choose

He'd call and tell you definitely

Put on your Blue Suede Shoes


Then he would tell you things

That would be important for you

And the biggest thing that he would say

Is you've Gotta Lotta Living To Do

# 27

# THE GREATEST SINGER EVER
## AKA ELVIS PRESLEY PART II

Elvis really was the best

Prepared for every occasion

If you were arguing with your lover

He'd sing A Little Less Conversation


If you were going on a date

Just to keep you out of harm

Elvis would call and tell you

Just wear your Good Luck Charm


If you're having problems in your life

Elvis would set the rule

He'd call and tell you sweetly

Come on now Don't Be Cruel

. . .

If you're not happy with your house

And all your friends said ditto

He'd call you all to tell you

Thank god you're not In the Ghetto


If you are having problems

Just talk to the man above

He'd just get Elvis to call to say

That you Can't Help Falling In Love


If you're worried after the weekend

Cause you got an awful fright

Elvis would say don't worry

Because it was Such A Night


If you're arguing with your partner

But you know they are always kind

Elvis would get you to whisper

You are Always On My Mind


Come on now just get ready

I know you'll have a sup

Cause when you meet your new love

They'll sing I'm All Shook Up


Finally in your love life

Think always Love Me Tender

And if you row and write to apologise

Make sure it doesn't get Return To Sender


If you are trying to fix a problem

And you know it probably won't

Get sorted in time for everyone

Then Elvis would just say Don't

# VI

---

# COVID

# 28

# STRANGE

Strange times

As never seen before

And hopefully never again

Forever ever more


Strange places

Everywhere we go we see

Please keep at least two metres

Between you and me


Strange faces

Don't have a mask you fail

If you wore them in times gone by

You'd finish up in jail

. . .

Strange eyes

Like I've never seen before

The colours of the rainbow

Peering out from every door


Strange lives

We always acted kind of fair

Now all we ever, ever see is

Wash your hands signs everywhere


Strange safety

In hospitals sanitisers hang on every door

Now all places will have them

Hanging forever more


Strange future

Are these rules here to stay

Or will our lives go back to normal

In some near future day

# 29

# POSITIVE

EXCEPT IN COVID, NEGATIVE

Positive is a great, great word

It helps you going forward

Be always sure of what you are doing

And don't ever be a coward


My mother told me years ago

Be smart be sure be positive

And always keep those thoughts with you

For as long as you will live


But life goes on and sorrows come

And they'll keep you on your toes

If troubles come be positive

That's how the story goes

. . .

But now that Covid's come around

And lots of people tested

Positive is not the result you want

Cause you'd end up being rested

In illness going through one's life

Positivity is what you need getting a test

But negative is the answer

That will set your mind at rest

So positive and negative

Are important in each sphere

But it depends on the situation

Which one you want to hear

In health testing negative is good

But in most cases positive is the word

You want to hear and take on board

I know this sounds absurd

But positive is a great asset

As you progress on through life

Be positive bright and happy

Will keep away your strife


In most aspects of our life

Be positive and be caring

It will help you get to where you are going

And the children that you are raring

# 30

## LOCKDOWN
### AKA ORGANISE YOURSELF

Lots of people are having problems

With what's now well known as lockdown

And plenty of them are worried

Causing them to frown


But sure I don't know the reason

Why everyone is so sad

Cause lockdown in this present time

Is really not so bad


Think back to your forefathers

Who when their work was done

They went back home and had some food

But excitement they had none

．　．　．

They didn't have electricity

Or WiFi for the net

They didn't have computers

So no entertainment did they get


They didn't have mobile phones

So no contact with the world

Their main excitement nightly

Was laying in bed all curled


So come on and open up your mind

There's so much to do now

Just take the time to organise

And figure out just how


With Netflix and Sky Movies

There's so much for you to see

There's a wealth of entertainment

Just waiting for you and me


So treat this lockdown with respect

It's required to keep us healthy

So get organised and enjoy yourself

It's better that than to be wealthy


So get some wine and minerals

A load of popcorn, do bring in

Just pop them in the microwave

And have a family movie night in

VII
---
TRUMP

# 31

# TRUMP

You know you have a good name

If your second name is Trump

As long as you behave yourself

And don't act like a chump

You'll have the whole world at your feet

If in business ventures you pump

And your looking after everyone

And your second name is Trump

But if your friends annoy you

From your team you'll make them jump

You will always get away with it

Cause your second name is Trump

. . .

If your first name is Donald

And your feeling out of luck

You are in the wrong position

And your second name should be Duck


If you are a US soldier

And you are sitting on your rump

Your first name is probably Forrest

And your second name is Gump


Now if your personal assistant

Is giving you the hump

You'll probably fire him from his job

If your second name is Trump


If your working at the Whitehouse

But your living in a dump

Just reach out to Donald

Cause his second name is Trump


So if your worried about your future

And you're looking for a lump

You have a big chance to succeed

If your friends with Donald Trump


But sometimes he doesn't listen

And he is rolling in the muck

He should just go and change his name

He should be Donald Duck

## 32

# DONALD TRUMP

### AKA THE BLEACH BLONDE AKA I'M PEACH 2

There was a US President

His name was Donald Trump

Unfortunately for everyone

He became an awful grump


He had a brilliant head of hair

His was bleached blonde

But the problems he encountered

Turned some supporters to abscond


He groomed his hair quite often

Every few weeks at least

But the colours got mixed up

And he became a beast

．．．

I saw his rubbish some months back

His hair box was Peach number 1

I think the roots went to his brain

And his sanity was gone


Just a few short weeks ago

I found the box again it's true

The colour it was different again

This time twas Peach number 2


This event it was so wrong

The colour got to his brain

He did some things he shouldn't have

He turned his followers insane


They tried to storm the senate

To get him back in power

He urged them to persist

And they listened, what a shower


But I've discovered the reason

And I'm about to tell to you

He might be blonde outside

But inside he is Peach 2


So he said that he was sorry

And that he didn't mean to do

He said because my hair is blonde

Inside my head I'm Peach 2

VIII

---

# ADVICE & HELP

# 33

# LSW

LIMERICK SUICIDE WATCH

The team at L S W

Are a mighty, mighty crew

A fabulous group of volunteers

All doing their best for you


They go out on the river banks

They watch the whole night long

Waiting to be there for you

If you're not feeling strong


I really love just what they do

Their thoughts are true and true

Always watching carefully

And always there for you

So if you're feeling worried

And not sure what to do

There's always a solution

There's always something new

If some things are hard for you

And you don't know where to go

I hope you meet the LSW

Because they will love you so

They'll help you with your problem

And guide you on your way

They will also help you plan your life

Through each and every day

So keep this info by your side

And if you ever need a lift

I hope you'll talk to the LSW

Because they'll give you a gift

. . .

They'll give you back your freedom

And help your life get good

And lead you to the future

To live life as you should

# 34

# FR ANDREW MULLIN

Andrew Mullen is a special man

I got to know him quite late

When I got a chance to check his story

Sure it buckled up my Faith


He was a young man from Daingean

Who became a Catholic priest

But things didn't work out well for him

And soon his life was ceased


They buried him in Carlow

In a grave so far away

That the people back in Daingean

Wanted him buried in their local clay

·  ·  ·

They got their wish, he was dug up

To bring him right back home

There wasn't a blemish on his body

A miracle sure had come

In 1818 he passed away

Fifteenth January to the day

Now people come from far and near

To sit down there and pray

To me he is my special friend

From just three years ago

I heard his story on the radio

And I knew I had to go

Within a month I got there

I was as curious as could be

I was thinking of the many things

That hopefully he could do for me

So from that time I've been there

About six times every year

But I pray to him almost every day

Because I want him near


So if you're up there listening God

It would be worth it if you tried

You might understand his value

And have him Beatified


So Andrew please look after us

And all in our family tree

And just keep helping us along

Please keep us safe and free

## 35

# SHINE THE LIGHT

If you want to know where you're going

Then you need to shine a light

It makes things seem much easier

When the way in front is bright


It gives you so much pleasure

When you know what's in store

And you'll enjoy the journey

Really so much more


If you have a doubt about it

Then you need to find the way

Or you could end up in trouble

Like trying to find a needle in the hay

But things are always better
When you sit and make your plan
It makes things so much easier
For every woman and man

So keep those options opened
To really keep in sight
And the best way to do that
Is to always shine the light

If we go together
And I can depend on you
You'll always be there to guide me
And to show me what to do

Always be quite positive
And also be real bright
Always know where you're going
And always shine a light

. . .

So please remember and stay bright

And keep all good things in sight

Cause you'll never know when you might

Need to always shine the light

# 36

# MIGHT AS WELL SMILE

Life is awfully funny

Full of ups and downs

But if you meet some good ones

And not meet all the clowns


Now clowns can be quite funny

They'll fill your eyes with tears

Hopefully with happy things

And not with lots of fears


A lesson I was taught quite young

For health, run lots of miles

And also always fill

Your face with loads of smiles

. . .

Cause no matter how bad things get

Don't heap them in a pile

And remember always

That it's better to give a smile


Now if you're feeling down and out

And you're not sure what to do

It's always better to realise

That a smile is good for you


So think of something funny

That will make you laugh a lot

And remember all the good things

That give your life a shot


As you go along through life

And your plans some people spoil

Always keep your posture

And greet them with a smile


Now the moral of this story

By a massive country mile

Is that the best way to live life

Is to always have a smile


So when you're feeling down and low

Don't let things get to boil

And to live your life in harmony

You really need to smile

# 37

# MANNERS

When you meet some people

You know if they are good

They'll talk and act quite pleasantly

As people always should


Now some people are just different

And they don't have a care

So when they are with others

Their manners are quite bare


When I was young my mother said

When you want something say please

And others will always like you

So to smile always think, cheese

. . .

She said when you're given something

Be sure to always say thanks

And don't be rude to anyone

Because they'll think you're cranks


I tried to do what she said

To always be polite

Sure it got me here to where I am

And my mind was always right


Now my kids are grown-up

I think we did do well

To train them to be nice always

And to their friends do tell


Tell them that it's good manners

To always have a smile

And be good friends to those you love

And help them for a while


Always say to someone please

And they'll give you what you want

And definitely always say thanks

Even when you think you can't


Please do teach your children

To be polite and have less strife

It will help them on their journey

Always throughout this life

# 38

## STRESS

I was always doing sporty things

And I was always fairly fit

And that just kept me going

I was never worried one bit


Back then I was young and carefree

And always playing sport

And went away for work sometimes

And was often in an airport


Flying didn't bother me

And nothing caused me stress

I really did enjoy life

And I lived at my address

But life goes on and years fly by
And health and age progress
And things that never bothered me
They now fill me with stress

I pick myself up and carry on
And continue what I'm doing
And hope the stress gets better
And that my worries just get going

People say relax and calm yourself
And let your troubles go
But sometimes that helps a lot
And often really no

If you're stressed with something
Let your good friends know
And sure they'll rally round you
And help your troubles go

. . .

Always be prepared for it

And know what caused the mess

Get family and friends to help you

Get rid of all your stress

# IX

---

# VARIOUS

Today is just another day

I've been told all my life

But it often turned out to be

Filled with lots of strife


What no one seems to see

Is that it's very clear

If you need to do something good

That Today is always here


Yesterday it was Today

When we were back there then

But tomorrow will also be Today

If we ever get there, when

. . .

Now the most important message

Is if you've something to do

Then Today's the only option

That will be there for you


So the moral of this story

Is so clear in every way

The only day to do something

Will always be called Today

# 40

## CHASING DREAMS

All my life I had great plans

Always looking for the best

Always trying to get ahead

And stay in front of the rest


Some things work well and others don't

But you have to stay in charge

Often things don't work out well

And your loss might be quite large


Some big things that I dreamed for

Really worked for me

Like the round of golf in Shannon

When I scored that 63


But then when I was training

I let my focus slip

I kept on trying to get fit

Until I did in my hip


Life is full of ups and downs

And people chasing dreams

Some things have a joyful ending

But others end with screams


Just always try your level best

You sometimes will succeed

As some will end disastrous

Because of someone else's greed


Never lose your focus

And always plan ahead

Lots of things will work for you

Sure some will end in dread

.   .   .

Always, always chase your dreams

And some will work for you

But the fun that you create

Will last your whole life through

# 41

## SUNRISE

It depends on where you are to see

What happens at sunrise

You'll see magic sights develop

Right before your very eyes


When it's on the way to visit

The sun will let you know

The skies will change its colour

And start a big bright glow


Then the sun comes out

It bursts right into view

And then starts great sights

How, I haven't a clue

. . .

It all looks different wherever you are

But the one I thought was grand

Was when we were on holidays

And I was standing on the strand


The sun appeared from behind a hill

And just above the sea

The view was so spectacular

I thought oh my, oh me


But then some clouds did gather

And the picture changed again

And I thought twas great to be here

And I prayed to God Amen


Sunrises are quite beautiful

When the sun gets to peer through

It gives us lots of pleasure

To both me and you


It doesn't matter where you are

On land or hills or sea

The sights that I see every morning

Will live in my memory


Here's to every sunrise

May it help you make your peace

And each day you see the sunshine

Will help your troubles to cease

## 42

CONCENTRATE

When I was young my mother said

Always take care of what you are doing

Don't try to think of other things

Cause there might be trouble brewing


Do what you are doing and do it right

Be sure to concentrate

You'll always get the job done

And then you can celebrate


So many people lose their thoughts

And forget the job in hand

Sure it often doesn't work out good

And not the way twas planned

If you think that you know everything
And your work will be okay
Don't let your mind wander too far
That's for another day

If you do the job you're doing
And be oh so correct
You'll get it finished in good time
And then your pay collect

If you wander in your mind
And forget just what you're doing
As I said before and now again
It's just your troubles brewing

Lets be fair to everyone
Especially the one that's paying
Concentrate on the job in hand
Don't let your mind go straying

. . .

So my mum God love her

She was so right

She said just concentrate fully

And your future will be bright

# 43

# MULTITASKING

Multitasking is something cool

That only women can do

Or if I believe my missus

Then it surely must be true


A man can only do one task

But mainly gets it right

But a woman can do many things

But not all will turn out bright


My mum told me a long time ago

When you want something done well

Don't be multitasking cause

Your task might look like hell

. . .

If you do one thing at a time

And do it really right

You'll always keep that task

In your mind and in full sight


Only women can multitask

Or if the truth be told

It's in their mind they can't do wrong

And if you disagree you're bold


When your missus tells you

Just one job at a time

Just tell her fine it's ok

She can do the rest that's fine


So remember this forever

Only women can multitask

Don't try doing more than one job

Unless you've a woman's mask


To be honest I must tell you

One job at a time is good

And all men should consider

Only do one if you would


Cause if you try to do more

Without wearing a woman's mask

Your wife will quickly tell you

Sure you can't multitask

# 44

## RAINBOWS

It's been always with me

Since the day I first saw light

Was the colours of the rainbow

And them shining oh so bright

I was amazed to see them

Pop up throughout my life

Sure they used to ease my worries

My troubles and my strife

That time I saw the first one

My mind was filled with glee

And on my journey through life

They filled me with ecstasy

· · ·

Thank God I had a camera

And then a phone that took

Photos of many rainbows

To have in my photo book


Then we heard a story

Twas about a pot of gold

They could be found at rainbow's end

At least that's what we were told


So all my life I tried to

Find this rainbows end

A pot of gold would be so nice

To my family I could send


Lots of lovely presents

Bought with my pot of gold

But I never ever got there

The truth sure must be told


Every time I got near

The end just moved away

So I never got to the rainbows end

From then to this present day


I have lovely photographs

Some like you've never seen

They are just like things you'd see at night

In the middle of your dream

# HOMETOWN

My hometown is a special place

It's the town where I was born

The first time that I saw the light

Was nine forty five one morn


I lived my early life there

Grew up with some great friends

We schooled and played together

And planned our future trends


I had some early tragedies

While living my young life

But friends were always there for me

To help me through the strife

. . .

As we grew up we drifted

To places far and near

But we always kept in touch

Almost each and every year


But then we met our partners

Some were from the town

Then some drifted far away

To live and settle down


Eventually that came to us

And we had to go away

To work and live in foreign parts

So that we could earn our pay


We came back to our country

But not to our home town

We had a lovely family

We learned to settle down


We're gone now from our home town

But we never will forget

The life we had as youngsters

And the great friends that we met


Now our time in life is here

And we are really settled down

But I never ever will forget

Sweet Thurles my hometown

# 46

## LAUGHS AND GIGGLES

It's so funny when you hear it

That's people having fun

Whether sitting home and giggling

Or just going for a run


Some people laugh and giggle a lot

And are always in good humour

No matter what the story is about

Or no matter what the rumour


They're really happy quite a bit

If they laugh and giggle a lot

Some times they just keep smiling

The past never to be forgot

. . .

But it's nice to see some people

Who are happy with each other

To find someone who always

Gets on well with your mother


Laughs and giggles are better

Than sitting there in pain

And life goes on no matter

And sure must be lived again


So laugh and giggle all the time

To me it just sounds great

To hear two people so happy

And always in a good state


Now crying is the other option

It's not good for anyone

No matter what the story is

And no matter what has gone


Be happy laugh and giggle

Many friends are all around

Life will progress on for you

And new friends that you've found


This is the end of the story

Just laugh and giggle out loud

And you'll always have good company

No matter who's in the crowd

# 47

# HUG AND KISSES

Hugs and kisses have been with us

All our whole life long

But I never thought how good they were

Until Covid came along


This virus is so destructive

It's like a massive bug

You don't realise how bad it is

Until you can't give your grandkids a hug


Hugs are so important

To show friends that you care

It can mean so much to someone

When with them a hug you share

. . .

It's been so long since Covid came

Will it ever go away

When we can hug family and friends

Hopefully soon someday


Do what you are let do

Show them that you are there

Let them know how good they are

And that you really care


Don't get too disappointed

The light at the end is near

When we can hug our grandchildren

And rid them of their fear


Vaccines are here at present

The work is slow but sure

And as I said so earlier

The light at the end is the cure


So let's be patient for a little while

And imagine that hugs are real

So that when we get to give them

Our friends,our love will feel


Let's be getting ready

Practice our hugs and kisses

Sure t'will help us going forward

And hopefully end all our blisses


All my grandchildren get ready

Cause big hugs are on the way

Hopefully this will be the start

Of big hugs and kisses every day

# 48

## SHARE

This is the most important word
Ever to be invented
It's the word that's there to help us
Get ourselves and others contented

If you have good will and fortune
And lots of riches at hand
Don't be afraid to share them
With all throughout this land

Because what you share with others
Will bring karma to your life
And your fortune will be safe
No matter what kind of strife

Then if you are troubled and lonely

And you're not sure what to do

Just share your problem with your friends

And they will be there for you


If you've helped someone in need

And you helped them get along

They will be there when you need them

They'll help you get back strong


To share is so important

Whether it's good or bad

A problem shared is a problem halved

And will stop you getting sad


If you share your good will

This will come back oh so good

And the help you give to others

Will only be as it should


This big word called share

Is a massive positive word

And should be used by everyone

And share what you can afford


Listen now and do things right

Share what you have to give

And always remember to do this

For as long as you will live

# 49

# ACCEPT WHAT YOU HAVE

## AKA BE HAPPY, BE GLAD

If you are feeling bothered and jealous

That someone has more than you

Be careful it's not always clear

What you see might not be true


People you know might not show

The worries that they might fear

When they're back alone at home

They might often shed a tear


It's not always what it looks like

So be happy with what you do

It might not always feel cool

But there's way worse off than you

. . .

Money isn't everything

Although it helps you through some crisis

But it's not the be all solution

And it sometimes causes surprises


If you are feeling healthy

And also you're not poor

Don't be worried about what others have

And don't be looking for more


Your eyes can sometimes deceive you

And you see something that's not

Exactly what you think it is

And they might have an empty pot


Keep your expectations moderate

And accept things as they are

Will help you going forward

And will take you quite far


Everyone that you look at

Isn't always feeling right

And might have many problems

When everyone's out of sight


Be happy with what you have

And always really be glad

Because if you lost what you have now

You might have a reason to be sad

## 50

### ELECTIONS

Elections every four or five years

Are really full of ranting

People calling to your door

Offering you whatever you are wanting


You don't see them for a few years

They're busy collecting money

They shout a few times in the Dáil

They really think they're funny


They don't care what you ask for

They'll promise it to be

They'll tell you just get them elected

And then just wait and see

. . .

When they come a calling

And knock on my front door

I know the rubbish that they speak

Cause I really know the score


Some would offer you the lotto

If they thought t'would get your vote

Some would offer to sort your WiFi

Even though you are quite remote


And when the election is over

And your man he gets the cheers

Make sure you remember what he looked like

Cause you won't see him for years


And when the Dáil is in session

And they talk about past tenses

You can be quite sure in all the fuss

They'll never forget their expenses


So the moral of the story

Is to vote for someone you know

Will do the normal work well

And keep the country in full flow


Don't be listening to silly plans

As you know they won't be met

And when they go away from your door

They quite quickly forget


Be careful what you look for

As it might cause you some stress

But if it doesn't come to pass

Do worry, cause he won't fix the mess

# 51

# MANAGERS

Managers can be so important

In oh so many places

Keeping the workload ongoing

And the workers to their paces


They're often very shrewd people

Always knowing what to do

To keep their workers up to it

And running a happy crew


Sometimes they're in tight places

Between those above and below

Always trying to keep their heads

And the workers in full flow

．　．　．

They know to get the work done

They need to earn lots of respect

They need to be tough but fair

And always knows what to expect


They need to show the owners

That they can solve any riddle

That they are very capable

And will always hold the middle


Now the best managers that I know

Remind me of past great jugglers

They always manage to get it done

Despite having maybe some strugglers


One of the morals of this poem

Is managers juggle many balls that's true

But if they ever drop some

Make sure it's not their own two


So be up front with everyone

Both those above and below

It will definitely help you carry on

And keep the work on the go


If you have to make a decision

And you're not sure what to say

Lean a bit towards your bosses

As it's them who decide your pay

## 52
---
## IF


If all words were spelt backwards

The if it would be fi

And sure I thought I wouldn't care

Cause it would never bother me


If we could see the future

What would we really do

Sure could we make some big plans

To make all our dreams come true


If today was tomorrow

And yesterday was today

Would it really make a difference

In any special way

. . .

If we could live our life over

Would we change some things or what

Or would we just do the same

Whether twas right or not


If we had an opportunity

To change our destiny

Would we be able to cope with it

And live in harmony


If is a mighty question

That people use a lot

They often try to get a chance

To really alter the plot


If we didn't do something right

Would our future be secure

Or would everything be broken

Forever ever more


Then if we were allowed to change

Our plans after the event

Would we be oh so happy

And would our thanks be meant


So always please remember

It's only a little word

That could make a massive difference

If, it really is absurd

# ABOUT

When John Purcell went for a check up at his local GP's, he wasn't expecting to end up in a cardiac ward only hours later. Getting on in years and still as active as he was in his twenties, the words "blockages" and "bypasses" were a shock to all.

During his month long stay, he passed the days putting pen to paper and turning out this collection of poems about his time there, his family and just life in general.

Poetry from the Cardiac Ward is John's first published work.

Printed in Great Britain
by Amazon

65254978R00113